Legal & Disclaimer

The information contained in this book is not designed to replace or take the place of any form of medication or professional medical advice. The information in this book has been provided for educational and entertainment purposes only.

The information contained in this book has been compiled from sources deemed reliable, and it is accurate to the best of the Author's knowledge. However, the Author cannot guarantee its accuracy and validity so cannot be held liable for any errors or omissions. Changes are periodically made to this book. You must consult your doctor or get professional medical advice before using any of the suggested remedies, techniques, or information in this book.

Upon using the information contained in this book, you agree to hold harmless the Author from and against any damages, costs and expenses, including any legal fees, potentially resulting from the application of any of the information provided by this guide. This disclaimer applies to any damages or injury caused by the use and application, whether directly or indirectly, of any advice or information presented, whether for breach of contract, tort, negligence, personal injury, criminal intent, or under any other cause of action.

You agree to accept all the risks of using the information presented inside this book. You need to consult a professional medical practitioner in order to ensure you are both able & healthy enough to participate in this program.

Contents

Grab Your Free Marketing Materials Here

If you've been building a list, you should know that writing emails can be hard...

Especially when you want to write emails that convert to sales.

There is a super shortcut for you to make money online -- using proven emails (without you doing the writing).

There are 2 weeks of fill-in-the-blank emails you can use to promote any related internet marketing products you like! Put in your own affiliate links and earn all the commission.

Or use them to promote your own products.

Get the email templates set for free by clicking on the link below:

http://bit.ly/2kGOEDd

Introduction

I want to thank and congratulate you for downloading the eBook, *"Top lessons learnt from losing 30k in my quest to become an internet millionaire."*

The fact that you are reading this is proof enough that you have a good idea of online income and you are looking to make the best out of it which is a really great thing. My reason for writing this book is to ensure that everyone who has an interest in making money on the internet ventures into the journey with an open mind. This I want to achieve by sharing the lessons of my own experience after having lost 30k in my quest to make lots of money online.

I would want to emphasize the fact that this book will prepare you for a world of possibilities but also one with some challenges. When I made my decision to try making money on the internet, I wasn't really sure what I was getting into but I also had very high hopes. It has been a tough journey but one that allowed me to learn a lot and most importantly given me an opportunity to finally understand that success doesn't always come easy as we wish it to.

What is true is the fact that there are so many possibilities online and is therefore a place for everyone because whatever your skill is there is something that you can do online and make some money. It is really gaining popularity as many are opting to work from home instead of having an office job and there are also those who are looking to make some passive income and they find online jobs the best option because it comes with numerous benefits.

In life it is always best to allow ourselves learn from our mistakes instead of allowing the mistakes we make from time to time to define who we really are or to prevent us from making another step to success. This is why I want you to go through all the lessons I learnt because I believe that it is going to help you have a deeper understanding of what it takes to be a success with online income.

This will actually put you a step ahead in the game and it will allow you to know where to put efforts and what caution to take. The best thing is that online jobs are for true and all you need to do is learn of the basics that will make it your shot to become a millionaire. I assure you that it has been quite a journey but one that is worth it because personally I believe that there is no easier way to make money than through the internet. The lessons will help you know some of the things to indulge in and also how best to handle the jobs you get.

We all always encounter obstacles in life and make so many mistakes but what makes you standout is the ability to learn from the mistakes that you make and overcoming the obstacles by not quitting. This book has been written in an easy to understand manner and it is my hope that the lessons learnt will enable you to grow as it did to me.

Chapter 1: My 2 Cents

MY THOUGHT ON MAKING MONEY ONLINE

When I first heard of online income and online jobs, I knew that this was the way to go for me because the deal was definitely too good. Who wouldn't want to make lots of money just seating on their couch? I really loved the fact that the internet offers opportunities to everyone without necessarily demanding for specific qualifications. I knew it takes a lot to be a millionaire but my mind somehow told me that with online income this is quite different because I could do as much work as I could and that it was just as easy as it sounded.

Most of us usually hear the success stories and focus only on the fruitful part of the story forgetting that there is always the trying and failing which is what gives the success more value. If I were to begin today with online jobs, I am sure I would have done a number of things differently because I now understand that it is not all about putting all your resources into something you have no understanding of but rather taking the time to analyze it critically. I had to learn this painfully as I lost 30k trying to be a millionaire.

Yes you can become a millionaire through the internet and yes you can be a real success but whatever you do I would really advise you to do it with an open mind. Before accepting my failures as a learning experience I believed that I had messed up big time. There is however that part of me that kept me strong and made me understand that apart from drowning in self pity why not get back to the drawing board and find out why things went wrong and how I could have done things differently. This is what led me to writing this book which I believe is going to be very beneficial to you as it is an analysis of the lessons that I learnt.

There are so many ways that one can make money on the internet but there are also so many things that you should be aware of before you make your first step. Online dollars require so much of you including persistence, hard work, discipline, patience and dedication. My first advise to you is that if you are going to give up at the first hurdle then it is better you don't start. I won't tell you it is all difficult because it isn't and all you need to do is to prepare yourself by learning the basics and effective tips for success. It took me time to know which exactly was the right way to go but all in all am glad that I was finally able to learn because I have a new approach to everything which is great and fulfilling. The best decision I ever made was choosing to stay motivated and making my experience a learning ground.

When you are working on the internet the most important thing you need to know is the best way to make money online is to learn how to expand your sources in the most effective way possible. It is also very important to make sure that your income is legitimate and honest.

The following parts of this book will take you though the main lessons that I have learnt when it comes to making money online. I will hold nothing back and I will give you the details on how to best handle yourself and also enlighten you on effective tips that will ensure you don't end up losing your shirt when you are starting out. Make it your life changing opportunity by understanding every single bit of information laid out for you.

Chapter 2: Lesson One - Focus

FOCUS

When I started working online I thought putting my finger on every single kind of opportunities was the best way to increase my earnings which was very wrong because everything you engage in needs a lot of concentration and when you are doing everything you lose focus. This is a key aspect when it comes to succeeding on the internet realm because it will allow you to efficiently distribute your resources and efforts. Being a jack of all trades might take your mind off that one specific thing that you would have highly excelled at.

As I began I wanted to do everything from blogging to affiliate marketing. I wanted to publish on kindle, build a site but this I came to learn bitterly was a very wrong idea. When you want to succeed then you should ensure that it is a step by step journey. What I didn't do is give myself time to know exactly what I really wanted to and is the reason I was trying out everything I thought sounded good. In life we are always advised that to get to the level of success that we aspire, we need to take some time to determine what we want first and strategize on the best approach to take. By this I mean there was no way I was going to publish on kindle, engage in marketing, build websites and at the same time be a blogger.

When you jump from one thing to another you might end up not getting much because a specific item may need a lot of focus and it can become taxing at times. When you focus on one thing you make it easier for customers or employers to see you as the person who is great at what you do. By this you will even find it easier to work as not much will be required of you. If you are looking to do a number of things then it is best that you first specialize on one and when you are really good, and actually making some money out of it, then you can try your hand at something else.

Passion is always a key weapon to success and it is not possible to be passionate about so many things. Passion and focus always go hand in hand because they are both a source of motivation and will keep you on track. The question that I finally asked myself was would I prefer being good at so many things or being great at just one thing and this allowed me to make the right decision.

To build focus you must first begin by identifying your areas of interest as I did and find out all about it before you try it out. This way you will have a deeper understanding of what you are getting into and are therefore less likely to make mistakes. The lack of focus causes a lack of real progress in any one particular direction and can lead to failure. The worst thing with lack of focus is that it usually leads to scattered resources and you might end up wasting a lot of time handling so many things with no real benefits

Chapter 3: Lesson Two-Paid Advertising Are Not For Beginners

PAID ADVERTISING ARE A CROCK OF SHIT...FOR BEGINNERS

Many people by now know that companies such as Google and Facebook use all the information you give them to build a personalized internet experience for you. Most people using these sites usually know that they keep records of all the things you do and use it to create a profile of the type of person you are. Most of us know this but we just don't like to believe it. When you check your Google Ad preferences, you will be surprised because when you are still signed into Gmail account Google knows your gender, age, language and what you are interested in. Google will use this information to modify your internet experience and as you move around the Google Display Network you will be shown ads that reflects your interest. You know all of this and I know you don't like to be reminded of it. Most of us feel the same way. This is how they allow advertisers to target by demographics and interest.

Nevertheless, if you are new to internet scene, you should stay away from Google and Facebook ads. These ads are money sucking and a lot of campaigns usually need testing and modification before deciding to use them. If you are not well capitalized and well informed, my advice to you is that you shouldn't spend any money in useless campaigns as it may exceed any revenue that you can potentially bring in. I spend close to 4K on Facebook ads until my bank account goes dry. When it comes to ads you should be a step ahead and make assumptions on which words users are likely to look for. Pay per click (PPC) is not the best way to advertise your business, attract more customers and grow your online business if you are not well capitalized. Though it has many benefits, it can result in great costs if not carried out appropriately, sensibly and responsibly.

Nowadays, Google is very expensive as compared to what it used to be a few years back. Keyword competition is becoming fierce and most general keywords associated with many businesses are very expensive. The Cost Per Click (CPC) for popular keywords such as "build a website" rangers from $4 to $8. This forces you to start being creative, making assumptions, and focusing on keywords with low competition where their Cost Per Click (CPC) ranges from $0.4 to $3. On Google, you are given the option of either displaying ads only on the search network of Google or through display partners. The results of the search and display network of Google can be poor if you do not know what you are doing. All you need to know about Google ads is that it is costly and complex, but has a very strong reach. It can be the best method for you if you have a unique and popular services or products but not when you are starting out with no solid ideas.

The cost of Facebook ad is comparable to that of Google but many people feel like Facebook ad is not better than Google. Facebook is a place of play and leisure and most of the time people go log in into Facebook to pass time or view comments and photos of others. Facebook users will not likely click on your add or even like your business. They might just skim over it and continue with their business.

Generally, Google and Facebook ads are capitalizing on advertising and many companies actually pay to reach a huge targeted audience, believing that they can get more customers and grow their business. What they may not be aware of is that policies change very fast and results are dependent on your creatives. It is not uncommon to see your ads ignored by user. You are required to pay by either views per page or clicks to the ad. This is a total waste of money and a very ineffective way of advertising. We are all looking for passive income but it is important for us to always look for the best method that can generate income.

Chapter 4: Lesson Three-Silver Bullets Do Not Exist

CHASING SHINY THINGS IS A COMPLETE WASTE OF TIME

Every little time that you save up is precious; therefore, stop spending too much time online looking for a new job and reading information on new products on arrival. There are new technologies propping up every day and staying away can leave you feeling detached and empty. To keep up with the speedy changes, one would decide to sign up with a list of gurus to receive updates on the latest IM news on the areas of interest. I am sure you have done this at some point in life if not often, but what can I say? Of course the economy is getting harder every day but that does not mean you can throw away prudence.

Every day you see new software being pumped out in to the open market. It comes with very interesting offers, new idea and many people in your social class are aware of it being the most recent cath. The software comes from most trusted companies and institutions with a mark in revolutionizing daily activities. And they tell you that you can make gazillion dollars by using their software.

The product seems interesting, and the promise of a million dollars seems attractive. So, you purchase the software online. What they did not tell you is that they are making money off you by selling you the product. This is probably what you will never know not unless someone takes time to put this in your head. How many of these online products have you found to have been marketed in a similar manner, why are they similarly attractive with no risk attached? Can you run simple calculations and see how much they have made from selling products to people like you. Just imagine the number of people who have come across it. Keep in mind that some of them are online products that you may not even understand

Think about it, how can you make thousands using different products every day? I once receive an email from a guy who was promoting affiliate marketing on Tuesday, Amazon on Wednesday and later blogging on Friday. The products are totally different from one another. If you are not careful enough you may end up signing for similar product without knowing as many affiliate marketers push out products around the same time period.

Chapter 5: Lesson Four-Track Thy Money

ALWAYS TRACK YOUR EXPENDITURE AND TRACK WHICH CHANNEL BRINGS YOU THE MOST MONEY

As you start out with online income it is very important that you maintain the habit of tracking how much money you are putting in and how much money you are making. This is something I didn't really put in mind when I was starting out and I ended up spending so much but I never got anything out of it. Just because of this simple knowledge I lacked, my success with online income was compromised. In whatever area of life when you have goals set you will always need to follow through every step and find out whether you are on the right track or not.

When it comes to online income it is important for one to have short-term and long-term goals. These goals will help you to stay on track and you will be able to spend within your means. After you have set goals the next step is to analyze and evaluate which channel will bring you most income. Make sure you go through each channel and verify that the one you have chosen is not a scam. Nowadays, there are many scammers who know their way around online income, they have sites that might appear genuine but their main objective is to get money out of your pocket. It therefore important to find the best channel that is genuine and that can bring you most income.

Another important thing is budgeting; this will help you to allocate a given amount of money to a specific activity, such as online, food, fees, bills etc. Budgeting will help you to know exactly where your money goes and know if you are going to get a return on it or not. There is no need to spend money on a channel that can't generate income because your main objective is to get passive income from the channel you are investing in. If you find that a given channel isn't working out according to your expectations then you can choose another channel but make sure you do your extensive research and analyze it from every angle.

You should also keep in mind that some of the online income jobs don't require you to pay a fee. As you look for a channel that can suit you and find one that wants you to pay before you start working, make sure you evaluate if it is legitimate or not. Being cautious and a little skeptical can help you avoid unnecessary mistakes.

As said earlier, having many online income channels isn't the answer to getting more money and being successful. In fact, this will make you more confused, to lose focus and not to pay attention on basic things that can make you succeed. It is very easy to track your expenditure and know which channel is bringing more money. All you need to do is spend more time learning and understanding all you need to know about online income. Then start analyzing each channel and do extensive research on the possible income of each of them. You can also consult online experts about the type of channel you want to invest in before starting to put your money there. Say you run a fitness site and you spend some money doing blogging, videos and email marketing. If email marketing brings home the bacon, you should be spending more time there.

Chapter 6: Lesson Five – Guaranteed Sign Up Is A Waste of Money

SOLO ADS AND GUARANTEED SIGN UPS ARE FOR SUCKERS

Building a list is very important and I believe you have heard of it from time to time. The internet world had grown and become extensive with people promising to give you a certain number of subscribers or they guarantee a certain number of clicks. You are required to pay these people by the number of clicks or sign ups you get. Sure, you will probably see the number of subscribers increase but in general those are just freebie seekers and they never buy anyway. To make the matters worse, I once paid 500 bucks for just 1k subscribers but got scammed because it all came from the same IP address.

Guess what, you need to know that you are the customer to these solo ads and guaranteed sign up vendors. It is a slingshot of shit whereby people grow their number of subscribers to then sell them off for clicks. There isn't any business going on. Think about it, will big companies sell clicks from their subscribers? They never do that and so why should you.

Solo ads do guarantee how they have been tested by 3rd party, impartial traffic testers who are their customers and that they have recommended it. They even assure you that you can get thousands of customers. All these are just to grab your attention and make you to give them more money in exchange for more subscribers who you might think are genuine customers. Solo ads can also guarantee every one of clicks but what they don't tell you is that they usually change your solo ad to be as blind as possible so that they can increase the number of clicks. You should always remember that they guarantee clicks but not conversion. After you have bought a solo ad and they deliver the clicks, you might think your page sucks because the conversion is poor but the problem may not be you all. If you are buying a solo ad it is important to know that nothing is guaranteed and do not assume you are going to get sales. You will be sorely disappointed.

You might see some solo ads get a lot of positive reviews but if you investigate, you will come to realize that these reviews aren't genuine at all. These sites just fill in fake sign ups and clicks to make you believe that they can make your business grow. Many people get excited to get many subscribers but they don't try to make sales or even track sales. They also don't look at the IP address of where those leads really came from. If you want to use solo ads, make sure you are getting from a buyer's list.

Another thing about solo ads is that their opt in rate keeps on varying from about 20% all the way up to 70%. There is a generic swipe that is being mentioned and if you ask to opt in to their list and try to check it out, they would just send you to a different list to which they send the original swipe when they run the ad. Another trick these people do to generate a maximum amount of traffic is to send q generic swipe that has multiple links to different offers.

Chapter 7: Lesson Six – Value Is King

PROVIDE VALUE BY GIVING SERVICE, INFORMATION AND ACTIONABLE CONTENT

There are many programs that exploit customers by making them spend all of their money on advertising and marketing. This program makes you spend thousands of dollars and later shows you how you can earn extra cash by bringing more people into the program; this means that later on you will be paid from the money that participants paid later. The main purpose for this is to bring more people into the same program and then making them spend their money on the same thing that can make both of you lose lots money. I think these programs are pyramid schemes out to make an easy buck. You should also keep in mind that these programs are dealing with many participants and all they are after is making profit through their advertisements and marketing services. There are times where you and other participants have the same web design layout and product but many people believe they must join the program because it is a common practice in the IM world or they follow their favorite guru.

Be smart and start making real money by providing services for people, such as publishing kindle eBooks, developing automation tool etc. In this world there is no shortcut to success, if you have the skills and expertise don't wait for programs to advertise and market them for you, try it yourself and have in mind the users you are targeting. When it comes to the internet you need to be creative and do a lot of research before deciding to join a certain program. You can provide value by giving users the service, information and actionable content they are looking for.

Believe in yourself and start making the right choices in life because you will never know the outcome until you try something out. There are many people who have started their own online business and by now are very successful. The first step is to connect with people through identifying and relating with them, this can help to increase your influence. If you want to become a valuable connector start by making meaningful connections, find out the most important thing to them, help them find what they are looking for, connect with other people, ideas, tools and resources and then finally follow up systematically. You will receive more if only you give more and the more value you add the better things become.

The advertisers and marketers know how to do their work perfectly especially when it comes to explaining to you how you are going to be rich after doing something. Their main objective is to market their selves and find many customers through convincing you to spend money on their sites and inviting other people to use their services. As you already know the aim of any business is to make profit and expand and that is what many advertisers and marketers are doing. Avoid giving such people money to advertise or market products for you and start doing it yourself. This is the first step towards realizing that you are able to do many things with your knowledge and skills.

Chapter 8: Lesson Seven – Budget Your "Education" Fees

SPEND MONEY WISELY ON SEMINARS

Lately the easiest way to make money off people in a simple least suspected way is by calling on and introducing seminars. The ever expanding market and the new trends of marketing is becoming more of a challenge, even the most competent person requires advice to cope up with such speedy changes. At this rate the importance of a seminar cannot be disputed. But how do we understand if the seminar is important to us? This call us to go back to rule no 1, focus. Seminar and seeking out the internet jedi who will turn your life around is the last piece in the puzzle. This is the option that you should take when all other options have no sensible direction.

With the ever changing economy having a sense of direction and a good plan before doing any business is becoming the key to success. Always know what you want to accomplish first before signing up for those seminars. Ask yourself: Is the seminar in line with your interest? Do you understand the kind of seminar you that you are attending?

To get a better grasp about seminars, we have to go a little deeper into it. When it comes to internet marketing there are 3 types of seminars: General, Trading and Make Money Online type of seminars. For serious business issues it is recommended that you do not have to spend any of your tome attending general seminars since they do not have an agenda that is viable for any business. In simple term do not waste time on general seminars as they do not help. They talk about shitty mindset shift and most of the stuff they introduce are super broad and general anyways. It does not have value for traders who are interested in a particular line of work.

In general seminars nothing is binding, they offer nothing specific; they use a lot of word to express simple terms. You can read this stuff for yourself then understand it better on your own. Trading seminars: Narrow down to what instrument you want to trade, two trading style at most and discard the rest. This is helpful in building a trading system, expanding knowledge and of course, creating links with other people who are dealing on the same products.

You can save money on online seminars by reading up on warrior forum but avoid buying anything. You also need to figure out what is best way you can to use to make money online, which can generate sustainable income. After you have done this, the next step is to follow a genuine guru which will teach one method that can help you get more money. The things you need to consider include; do I need to put in more money, is it newbie friendly, is it time consuming, is it one hit wonder or can be replicated, is the product differentiated? I lost most of my money signing up for rubbish courses that do not meet the checklist. It is important to have a checklist so as to confirm that everything you want is being met and also to make sure that it is not a scam.

Chapter 9: Lesson Eight – Avoid MLM

AVOID ALL FORMS OF MLM

Sure, the preview looks good. Future residual income check looks nice but no, the statistics are dismal. Less than 1% actually makes full time income from this, like 0.005? Most reps breakeven or lose money. In my scenario, I join an MLM company which offers membership discount on products. Points expire within one year and later I discover I have no use for the product. Roped in a friend and she lost money on the deal as well. Collectively, we both lost around 1.5K each. Yes, your upline will tell you that all is good, more rejection means you are closer to yes but dang, it never works that way. Too much work for too little reward. And how can you sleep well when your friend lost money on the deal. The mental stress is simply not worth it. People will tell you that their business opportunity is different but all shit smells the same. If it sounds too good to be true, it probably is.

Not all multilevel marketing plans are legitimate. Basically if the money you make is based on your sales to the public it may be legitimate but if it is based on the number of customers you recruit and your sales you make to them it might not be. As you know, multilevel marketing companies usually employ a network of people who are independent salespeople who sell products directly to people in their community.

With MLMs you may have to constantly recruit people who will work under you and those same people will have to sell and you will also have to sell and soon everyone will be selling the same thing. Why not venture into something that will actually benefit you and one that pays you back for your hard work. I have always viewed MLM as a tool to start a business inexpensively but it really isn't. What I came to learn is that the essence of an entrepreneur is creating something new and one that is innovative.

What I want you to know is that pyramids are an illegal practice that focuses on soliciting their members to recruit more members more than the actual selling of the product. The truth is that the primary source of income for its members is usually the number of members recruited. If the business model of a specific MLM is from selling products then upfront fees is not required. There is also the idea of being promised big money with little work. This is a complete fallacy. You will probably have to spend a lot of time trying to convince people who are not interested to take up your business opportunity. Oh, did I mention that most MLM now runs on a 3 way presentation where you will invite your upline to present the opportunity.

So, it is not only taking away your precious time. It is taking away your upline's time as well. How does that sound for big money with little work? Not too impressive, isn't it...

Special Bonus

To thank you for purchasing my guide, I have specifically prepared the bonus **"Operations Quick Money – Step by Step Guide to Your First $100"** report for you. This report will show you how you can start generating some residual income from your internet marketing endeavors.:

In this report, you will find:

1. How you can use the internet to generate residual income

2. Effective techniques to find highly profitable products to promote

3. How to drive web traffic for free

3. And Many More…

To access this special bonus, simply visit the URL below:

http://bit.ly/2kC8Ia2

Conclusion

It is my hope that this book was able to give you a deeper understanding of what online income is all about and how to avoid most of the common pitfalls that make beginners lose their shirt. There is always so much you need to learn before embarking on any business venture and it is my hope that this book gave you all the information you need regarding online income.

It is therefore your responsibility to put into practice all that you have learnt…or rather avoid the pitfalls I that mentioned, to prove that all the effort you put into reading this book was worth it.

Spend wisely, think before you leap and I certainly hope you do not have to burn through 30K like I did. In the end, whether you want to go for affiliate marketing, kindle publishing or e-commerce, stick to one strategy and milk it till it produces a full time income before looking at other things.

- Ken Chong

www.ingramcontent.com/pod-product-compliance
Lightning Source LLC
Chambersburg PA
CBHW070233210526
45168CB00020B/2203